PAUL WINKLER

Retirement Income

Retirement Income

Requests for information should be sent via e-mail to contact@paulwinkler.com. Visit paulwinkler.com for contact information.

ISBN 978-1-7379304-5-7 (Hardcover)
ISBN 978-1-7379304-6-4 (Paperback)
ISBN 978-1-7379304-7-1 (ePub)

Cover and interior design: Bryana Anderle (YouPublish.com)

Contents

Introduction

BEYOND THE SALES PITCH

One of the most frustrating things in retirement is trying to get straight information on how to set up a stream of income. Many of the places to which you might turn seem only interested in selling or advertising investment products. Mutual fund companies want you to believe they are the best choice. Insurance companies market themselves as the "safe" alternative. Magazines and the media position themselves as an "unbiased source"—all while accepting advertising dollars from investment providers. Even the company that handles your employer plan will have its own marketing angle.

The only way out is to understand a few key things for yourself. This knowledge will help you see beyond the sales pitch. Believe it or not, investing is not as complicated as it may seem. Much of what you likely already know about investment principles is correct. You only

Much of what you likely already know about investment principles is correct.

need to know how to best apply your knowledge. That's what I'm here to show you. Let's get started.

THERE ARE TWO STAGES IN YOUR FINANCIAL LIFE . . .

We begin our careers working for money. That's the life stage we spend most of our lives in. We exchange our time, talents, and knowledge for a paycheck in the world of work. During this time, we should set aside a portion of all that we earn for the future. That way, when the future does come and we enter the second life stage of not working, we can live off of our "deferred income." You want to choose not to spend it when you are working so that it's available to you when you are no longer working.

Some common tools for deferring income are qualified plans like 401(k)s, 403(b)s, and 457 plans or SIMPLEs, SEPs, and IRAs, to name a few. Some people don't have work-based plans but use "non-qualified" plans (brokerage accounts, savings, etc.) to build up a nest egg.

There are about as many answers to this question as there are financial advisors in the world, but you should avoid most of them.

The important question is how to distribute those assets in retirement so the income will last as long as you do.

THE PITFALLS

Unfortunately, many of the common strategies for retirement income are straight from a sales pitch and can have significant problems with them. So in this guide, I start by examining these common approaches and then explaining the issues with them. Through that process, you'll start to develop an understanding of how to think about retirement income.

The conclusion will be an overview of the approach we typically recommend. The insights here are grounded in rigorous academic research from many well-respected sources and even have Nobel Prizes behind them. But anyone can get the basic principles—that's why I call it a logical approach.

Once you understand the problems behind what typical retirement income advice is, you'll see why the academic approach makes so much sense. My goal is to help you understand this stuff so that you can feel confident about your retirement strategy and, as we like to say, "relax about money."

PITFALL #1

Live off Bond or CD Interest

One common strategy is to live off interest payments from government, corporate, or even municipal bonds. The idea is to draw only the interest payments and avoid touching the principal.

Here's the problem: interest payments can vary significantly as rates change in the marketplace. (Remember that rates are highly correlated with inflation.)

While this means you might get a bigger payout when inflation is hot, you could be in trouble if the purchasing power of the dollar drops.

For example, let's say you have $1 million in bonds that pay 6%. You start off with an income that sounds good: $60,000. Historically, the safest bonds (treasury bills) barely pay more than the inflation rate—typically less than half of a percent more. If you took all the interest as income and inflation is 5.5%, then your principal would drop in purchasing power to $945,000 (5.5% of $1 million is $55,000, and $1 million minus $55,000 is $945,000). If that were to happen, it wouldn't take long for your income to fall lower than your likely needs.

Interest payments can vary significantly as rates change in the marketplace.

You could drift into higher-paying bonds, but then you'd take the risk of the borrower defaulting and being unable to honor their payments at all. There can also be a whole new set of issues if the issuer of the bond is able to refinance if interest rates go down. This is referred to as "callability." This may leave the investor in a position where they can only reinvest the proceeds at lower rates. This is referred to as "reinvestment risk." It's like getting the rug pulled out from under you just when you stand to benefit.

PITFALL #2

Dividend-Paying Stocks

Another commonly used strategy for income in retirement is buying dividend-paying stocks. Dividends are the portion of a company's profits paid back to the owners, or stockholders, of the company. There are also mutual funds and exchange-traded funds (ETFs) that purchase stocks in companies with a history of paying consistent dividends. The idea is to live off the dividend payments without selling the underlying stocks.

Here's the problem: if the companies reduce their dividends—and this happens all the time—you may be without income.

Just because a company, or set of companies, paid dividends in the past doesn't mean they will do so into the future.

The economy may slow down, costs may go up for the companies, or tax law changes may make dividend payments less advantageous. Another issue is that high dividend-paying companies are often distressed. I know that sounds counterintuitive, but think of it this way: If the dividend is high, what is it high in relation to? The price. Low prices tend to be a sign that investors don't have much confidence in the company. Prices often go down in the stock market when confidence starts to wane. Does it make sense for a person nearing retirement to concentrate a large amount of their retirement money in distressed companies? No, probably not. These companies can—and often do—go bankrupt or discontinue their dividends to shore up the company's financial picture. And it can happen at any time, without warning. Not something you want to be involved in when you need a reliable source of income.

Another issue is that high dividend-paying companies are often distressed.

PITFALL #3

Annuities

The strategy of using annuities for income is complicated, leading to much of the confusion and contradictory information. To give clarity, it will be necessary to simplify a few aspects of this product. Making a blanket statement that annuities are always "bad" or "great" is a disservice because—while they are mostly used inappropriately—they can be a useful tool in several specific circumstances.

Here's the problem: annuities are often promoted as the panacea for all things retirement.

Let's look at a little history before diving into the pros and cons of annuities.

The first annuities were used in the Roman Empire, where Roman soldiers were awarded lifetime income, referred to as "annua," for their service. Today, immediate annuities can serve the same purpose. Here is a simplified example of the concept, which assumes no commissions, insurance company expenses, or interest. Let's say there is a seventy-nine-year-old female with a life expectancy of ten years. If she has $100,000 and wants to know that she will not run out of money, she could buy a fixed immediate annuity that will pay income until death. In this instance, the payment would be $10,000 per year. If she lives at least another ten years, she gets her money back. If she only lives two years (receiving just two payments of $10,000), then the rest of the money is gone. The profit for the insurance company would go to another person who bought an annuity but lived beyond their life expectancy. With an annuity, the insurance company takes the risk of someone "living too long."

Now that you understand the purpose, let's look at some of the problems with annuities.

INFLATION

Since most annuities have no cost-of-living increases built into them, one of the bigger problems is that inflation degrades the purchasing power of the payments. To illustrate, in the early 1980s, the median income for a household was just $16,830 per year. Try living on that now. If you want a COLA (Cost of Living Allowance) on these products, you must add it through riders, which significantly increases cost.

AGE

Here's another issue.

> *The younger you are when you buy the annuity, the lower your payout will be.*

Keeping with my simple example, if her life expectancy were to go up to twenty years, the payout would be $5,000 ($100,000 / 20 years = $5,000 per year). Therefore, it can be problematic for someone to buy such a product when they may have decades of life in front of them. In my over thirty-year career as a financial planner, I have recommended such a product only a couple of times—in instances where the person was nearly out of money, of advanced age, and needed the highest guaranteed payout available.

LACK OF CONTROL

Annuities are often sold as an accumulation vehicle for pre-retirees. This is where things get interesting and often misleading. These products are referred to as "deferred annuities" since the payout phase (annuitization) may happen sometime in the future. I say "may" happen because only 5% of people annuitize[1]. People don't like to lose control of their money.

In a pure immediate annuity, the principal (purchase payment) is exchanged for a promise by the insurance company to pay an income for life. Since this payment stops at death, many people balk because the money they've accumulated will not benefit their heirs or a favorite charity after they are gone. You sometimes see "I'm spending my kid's inheritance" bumper stickers, but in my experience, people's priorities and wishes tend to change as they age. What seemed like a good idea in their sixties may be very different from what they want in their eighties and beyond.

Some products are designed to overcome this illiquidity by allowing the annuity owner access to some of the money even if they annuitize. Recognize, however, that solving this problem only creates another—a reduction in your future income. With some contracts, even a single withdrawal can void income guarantees. No free lunch.

With some contracts, even a single withdrawal can void income guarantees.

1. Ben Mattlin, "Activating an Annuity's Income," *Financial Advisor*, September 1, 2019, fa-mag.com/news/activating-an-annuity-s-income-51227.html?section=47.

WHAT ABOUT GUARANTEES?

These products are often promoted as having guaranteed returns. The pitch goes something like this: "No matter what the stock markets do, you will only see your account go up in value." That sounds wonderful, but it's usually referring to some form of an income rider. Essentially, with an income rider, a second account is established within the annuity. One account is the amount you can receive if the account is cashed out—often called the "surrender value." That amount can vary significantly based on the returns of the underlying investments. The second account is often referred to as a "phantom account" since the money cannot be withdrawn. This is the value they use to calculate your future income. In other words, the "return" of this account is not based on any underlying investments—hence the term "phantom."

The phantom account creates the illusion of gain with no pain. The account may go to impressive values, but the insurance company is in control of the future income. And remember, you cannot withdraw this money.

Here's an example from a sales presentation I once saw. The advisor asked a simple question: "Which is better? A 5% guaranteed return or a 7% guaranteed return?" Of course, you would think that 7% is better. But then he showed how the product that

> The phantom account creates the illusion of gain with no pain.

paid only 5% on the phantom account actually paid more income. Why? The insurer decided how much income would be paid. The account value may be higher in one product, but the payout rate—or how much of the account they pay you as income—can vary. The account value was just a number on paper.

VARIABLE ANNUITIES

Some products allow for investing in accounts that are much like typical mutual funds—investing in various stocks, bonds, and other markets. These are referred to as "variable annuities." While these annuities can also offer some of the same guarantee features that can raise costs, the stripped-down versions can be useful in some circumstances.

For example, if someone has a high-cost annuity with gains above what they invested, they may be able to transfer money to a variable annuity with no tax consequences. This would only be done if the annuity is not in a retirement account. It is typically the no-load, or non-commission-based, variable annuities that allow the investor to avoid higher "mortality and expense" charges that eat into the accumulation value of the account.

Unfortunately, since there are no commissions payable, the marketplace is dominated by commission-based products.

Beware that financial advisors can market themselves as fiduciaries (people who must keep your best interest first) but take that hat off when selling commission-based products.

FIXED ANNUITIES

Another form of a deferred annuity is the "fixed annuity." This is the easiest to understand since the product will pay a set interest rate over time. How that interest rate is determined can vary. Some companies base their rate on the investment portfolio of the insurer, while others may pay different rates to different policyholders. The issue with this product is the lack of inflation protection available.

To overcome the inflation problem, insurance companies developed another product, the "index annuity." This version dominates sales presentations now, despite great uncertainty when it comes to returns. This product typically credits returns based on an index (like the S&P 500, the Russell 1000, or the NASDAQ) and is hampered by a variety of factors.

Stock dividends, which are a large part of the return of the index, are excluded. Returns are further reduced with caps. For instance, if the index goes up by 10% in a given month, with a 3% monthly cap, you would only be credited with a 3% return. The sales pitch is that you can't lose money when the market goes down. Quite often, however, the insurer will give full credit to negative returns in other months. As an illustration, if the next month sees the index go down by 3%, the company will remove all the gain from the previous month—even though the return of the index was positive over the two-month period.

The company may also hamper returns through a "participation rate." For instance, they may allow you to only participate in 60% of the market upside. If the index goes up 10% (excluding dividends), the return credited will be only 6% (60% of 10%). That can take away much of the return of the index that, historically, has provided protection from inflation. In other words, the returns of these indexed products are often closer to fixed products.

The returns of these indexed products are often closer to fixed products.

Some companies have attempted to overcome these objections by issuing products that don't have caps and/or they may suggest participation rates that meet or even exceed 100%. How can they do that? This is possible when the insurer retains the right to change the crediting strategy after the product is issued and sold. Talk about blind trust.

Insurers will often develop new products based on an investment strategy that would have worked over the past five or ten years. This is called "backtesting." A strategy that would have been successful over a short period of time would look good as an illustration in the sales brochure. The problem is that the short-term history of the markets rarely repeats. By the time the strategy fails, it's too late. The product was sold, and the commission was paid.

Keep in mind that these explanations are generic in nature. When the public objects to certain features and decides not to buy the product, the insurers go to work developing a new design without the objectionable feature. But they always take a benefit away elsewhere. It is like a sophisticated game of whack-a-mole. You say, "I don't like participation rates." "Okay," says the insurer, "we'll limit returns with cap rates." Then you say, "But I don't like that either." Then the insurer tells you, "Okay, we'll just leave the option open to change both of them after you already own the product." Insurance companies own big buildings for a reason.

The short-term history of the markets rarely repeats.

HOW DO THEY GET AWAY WITH IT?

At this point you may be thinking, *How can the financial industry get away with so much sleight of hand?* The answer comes down to regulation. In some countries around the world, it is illegal to provide commission-based financial advice.

In America, many believe that it is the buyer's responsibility to protect themselves and become educated about products.

It is "buyer beware" at its finest.

One recent study by the Council of Economic Advisors suggests that index annuities can cost savers $5 billion per year due to conflicting advice. Other studies have shown that many investment advisors *themselves* are confused about the downside of various investment strategies.

Many investment advisors themselves are confused about the downside of various investment strategies.

This often leads advisors to make mistakes with their own money. Unlike many industries, the barriers to entry into the financial world are relatively low. The tests required to call oneself a financial advisor may only require a few weeks of study. The education for financial designations is often provided by colleges funded by the insurance industry or indirectly funded by financial firms who pay for the education provided to their employees.

It is often said that it's hard to get people to change what they are doing when they are paid to do things as they've always done them. It's difficult to sell investments that may go up and down in value to a public that would prefer "all reward and no risk."

Rather than truly educating the investor and helping them understand how markets work, it's often easier to tell them that what they want exists.

If the commission payment is paid up front, the advisor may be long gone by the time the investor learns that they have made a mistake.

The promise to give stock market returns without risk is impossible when the insurance companies themselves are investing your money in the stock market. If they are taking that risk, then they must pass it on to you or put the company at risk. Have you ever noticed that the fine print of insurance illustrations always points out how the guarantees are based on the claims-paying ability of the company? If they mess up, they can become insolvent. The actuaries who design these products are good at math and are unlikely to put the company in that kind of danger. Instead, it tends to be the investors who bear the risk.

PITFALL #4

Target Date/ Balanced Funds

This approach to investing is a common default method in work retirement plans. The idea is this: investors are typically ill-informed when it comes to investing, and the mutual fund company is here to help. Instead of making investment choices on their own, the employee is given the option to hand this task to a professional. If your target date to retire is the year 2035, then all you have to do is choose a "Target 2035" fund. On the other hand, a balanced fund may be named for the level of risk that you want to take. For instance, the fund may be called a "moderate growth" fund.

In theory, this sounds good. The problem comes with implementation. Most investors fall prey to two biases that cause fund companies to invest in ways that can be counterproductive for taking an income throughout retirement.

The first is the desire to excessively focus on avoiding market risks.

As a reminder, if we avoid market risk, we can end up taking too much inflation risk.

This, as we've seen with living off interest, can cause a significant drop in purchasing power. This is a common complaint about target date funds. They often move from a heavy focus on stocks when the investor is young to a mix that is mostly bonds. Since people fear what they don't understand, they may feel a false sense of security with a portfolio mix heavily skewed this way.

The second issue is that these funds tend to focus excessively on big US companies. We tend to feel more comfortable when investing in companies familiar to us. They can also have lower visible costs since big companies can be cheaper to manage. The problem is that portfolios concentrated on narrow segments of the market tend to exhibit greater levels of volatility.

We tend to feel more comfortable when investing in familiar companies.

When a portfolio is more volatile, the odds of running out of money will often increase. When stock markets go down, an investor is forced to sell more shares of their stock to get the same amount of income. When they sell more shares, obviously, they have fewer shares that will benefit when the market recovers.

When it comes to investing, "one size fits all" often fits no one.

PITFALL #5

Life Insurance Retirement Plans

I thought this strategy had died a brutal death years ago, but it's back. During the 1980s in particular, interest rates were at all-time highs. Insurance companies—who invest mainly in bonds—started crediting higher interest rates in the products they sold. Agents would project rates of 8% or more on "fixed universal life insurance products," and the sales pitch would show how you could get a large tax-free income in retirement.

When someone is young, the cost of life insurance is low. So if you make a large payment, anything exceeding the insurance cost goes into an investment account that earns interest. When interest rates were high, insurance companies could make impressive projections.

I thought the strategy had gone away because the products sold in the '80s and '90s ended up severely underperforming due to steep declines in interest rates. To make things worse, the cost of insurance also went up for many of the products, which further hampered accumulations.

Here's the problem: interest rates are highly correlated with inflation rates. For example, if interest rates are 4% but the inflation rate is 3%, then my net return is only around 1%. Am I any better off if the interest rate is 9% and inflation is 8%? No. I'm still barely outpacing the rising costs of living.

Interest rates are highly correlated with inflation rates.

When inflation was high—as it was in the '80s—interest rates in these insurance products were high too. This gave a false sense of confidence about how much money there would be in the future. When inflation went down, so did the rates paid inside these insurance products, as well as the promise of high returns.

The other problem is that the cost of insurance goes up as we age. As we near mortality, the insurance company charges more for that additional risk. Just as you get to the point of taking an income from your life insurance policy, the cost of insurance starts to eat into your cash value.

If the policy runs out of money and lapses, the insured owner may have to pay more in taxes than what they put into the plan, which can be a nightmare.

Newer life insurance strategies, like indexed universal life, come with new problems. With indexed products, agents are often selling the idea that the buyer can get the tax benefits that come with life insurance, along with the gains in the stock market. These products often track popular indexes. The problem here is that they have reduced returns because they exclude dividends (profits paid back to shareholders) and only credit a percentage of the market's upside through "participation rates" or "cap rates." Remember: there is no such thing as a free lunch.

Typically, the products pay large commissions to the advisor and the firm they work for. There can be significant pressure on advisors to produce sales and hit the quotas set by their employers.

Why does the industry work so hard to get you to buy these products?

Life insurance was originally designed to replace income if the insured died prematurely. Beware when financial people try to convince you of its great merits in generating income for retirement. At the very least, get a second opinion (from someone not involved in the sales process) before signing on the dotted line.

Life insurance was designed to replace income if the insured died prematurely.

Real Estate

This option can appeal to many investors for a variety of reasons. Real estate can provide an income stream through rent payments, and the value of the underlying property can increase and potentially grow rental income in the future. It is often said that real estate is great because "they aren't making any more of it." However, that ideology is a bit misleading. While they may not be making more land (except in places like Dubai), new construction takes place on a regular basis. If supply outstrips demand, prices can drop significantly, and vacancies can become a problem. Tax law changes can negatively affect values as they did in the 1980s. An industry may move out of an area and affect demand for homes in that region—think Detroit and the car industry. Here's the problem: interest rates, work-from-home trends, tastes, local tax policy, or any number of factors can affect real estate values in unpredictable ways.

Investment firms selling real estate investment trusts (REITs) often advertise high yields and stable income. But they don't tell you that those things often disappear after the product is issued. To add insult to injury, many are "non-traded" and suffer from illiquidity since they are not listed or traded on public exchanges. This means that the investor may have to hope they can find a private buyer, should the investor want to sell. But if the yield has dropped, buyers will only be willing to pay pennies on the dollar.

One of the core tenets of investing is diversification. When an investor becomes too concentrated in real estate, or any other asset class, bad things can happen. I often avoid real estate in portfolio mixes completely—because companies (stocks) in the portfolio often give exposure to real estate already. Think of it like this, as Ray Kroc of McDonald's fame is often quoted as saying: McDonald's is more of a real estate company than it is a restaurant.

Conclusion

A Logical Approach to Retirement Income

When it comes to taking income in retirement, an approach that relies on a process, rather than a product, makes intuitive sense. This approach is backed by significant research on how markets price securities and balance the various risks faced by investors.

The approach is based on the concept of market efficiency and the factors that drive returns. Market efficiency is the idea that securities (like stocks and bonds) are selling for what they are worth based on knowable and predictable information. If a stock is selling for $50 a share, then that is what it is worth. This means that trying to get higher returns than what markets deliver on their own tends to be futile. In other words, the efforts of even the brightest on Wall Street to figure out which stocks are better than others or which markets will outperform next tend to hurt returns and increase risk. We've all seen or heard about monkeys throwing darts at the stock tables and beating the pros. It is very difficult to outsmart the market, and those who do don't tend to do so repeatedly.

Some market segments have delivered higher returns than others throughout history, and this needs to be considered in the design of your investment portfolio. For instance, some types of companies, like small or distressed ones, would logically have to pay more to use your money due to the risk involved. Just as you would charge more interest when loaning money to someone with a low credit rating, an investor will want to pay less for the right to receive the earnings of a company whose future may be questionable. That is the risk and return trade-off.

While entire books have been written, by myself and others, on evidence-based investing, I will simplify the approach for you here. Taking income from investments involves three processes:

1. Choosing assets to hold in the portfolio
2. Deciding what percentages to dedicate to those assets or market segments
3. Maintaining balances by taking income from those that have become overrepresented as time goes on

For instance, let's say we had ten market segments in our retirement account: large US stocks, small US stocks, large value US stocks, small value US stocks, large international stocks, small international stocks, intermediate bonds, short-term bonds, ultra-short bonds, and cash.

Now let's say that we decide to put 10% of our money in each of those areas. The stock assets may have expected returns, based on history, ranging from 10% to 14%, while the bonds may only be expected to return 3% to 6% over the long run. However, in any given year, some areas may go up in value while others go down. In years where stocks decline in value, bonds often hold their value or may even increase above average amounts. When stocks jump in value, bonds may have minimal return. Historically, at least one of the areas will go up in value during even the worst of economic conditions. When stocks recover, as they always have, the recovery can be fast and furious.

HOW DO WE TAKE INCOME?

This leads to how income is taken. If large US stocks have a great year, you might want to put more money into that area. However, we know that trees don't grow to heaven, so a more logical choice would be to *pull* income from that area. If we are supposed to have 10% of our money there and that area has just outperformed all the others, it will be taking up a higher percentage of the overall portfolio. If it represents 14% of our holdings, then we can sell some of those large companies, thereby bringing the overall portfolio back into balance. The next year it may be international small companies leading the way.

We hold more variable assets, like stocks, to help protect us from the ravages of inflation. Less variable assets, like bonds, are held to protect us from stock market fluctuations.

"WHAT IF I AM TOO OLD FOR STOCKS?"

A common concern amongst retirees is the risk of investing in stocks during retirement. You may worry that you don't have time to wait for a recovery if the market should drop. Or, worse yet, you wonder, *What if the market goes down and doesn't recover?* To answer these concerns, we need to understand a little bit about what causes downturns and walk through the consequences of a permanent downturn.

The first thing that I explain to people is the historical length and frequency of market declines. From 1954 through 2023, 5% intra-year declines happened approximately once per year and lasted 101 days on average. During that same time, 20% declines happened approximately every six years and lasted on average about 370 days. To protect against longer downturns, it is wise to hold several years of fixed-income investments (bonds). Downturns have always been temporary and, quite often, much shorter than people realize.

WHAT IF THE MARKET NEVER RECOVERS?

Let's walk through this concern. If that were to happen, that would mean that company earnings (market-wide) went down and never recovered. If that were to happen, then tax revenue would go down (or away) at the government level. If the government were to go away, then all your bank guarantees would too—and you would have a lot more to be concerned about. Insurance guarantees would likely be useless too, since the insurer's investments would be affected.

Keep in mind that companies will drop expenses (cost of supplies, labor, operating costs) to get back to profitability, even if they can't increase sales. Which is why I never sweat downturns in the stock market. Companies have many tools they can use to get back to profitability, and the financial system as a whole depends on their recovery.

Consider this: if stocks didn't have some volatility, they would provide no additional expected return. It is the additional return potential that, historically, protects investors from inflation. In fact, the income research referenced above found that optimal portfolios are at least 50% stocks when balancing the risk of inflation with market risks.

THE BOTTOM LINE WITH RETIREMENT INCOME

The amount of income that can be drawn on a yearly basis can vary based on factors such as age, asset mix, costs, whether or not income needs are flexible, potential for inheritances, and a number of other things.[2] It is more important, for the purposes of this guide, that you understand there is a significant amount of research out there. You don't have to throw your brain away when it comes to developing an income plan.

Discipline is key to making this approach work. Human nature is to panic and sell investments that have dropped in value or run to hot market segments after their time in the spotlight is over. Working with an advisor who educates while maintaining tight discipline is critical. If the advisor isn't well-versed in these academic processes, they may do more harm than good.

As you can see, there are a number of myths when it comes to taking an income in retirement. Avoiding commission-based investment advice is important because it can create significant conflicts of interest. While this guide isn't intended to cover every nuance of the retirement income puzzle, my hope is that it can help you recognize the approaches to avoid. Knowing what *not* to do is critical.

---

2. There has been a significant amount of research supporting 4% as a "safe" withdrawal rate from a well-designed portfolio. In other words, one can draw $4,000 per year from a $100,000 portfolio over any thirty-year period throughout history with an increase for inflation. This was originally promoted by the work of William Bengen and has been hotly debated in recent years. From my own personal experience, the failure of those who tried this approach and saw poor results was due to the failure to capture market returns and the holding of bonds with significant interest rate risk.

Education is key. The more you understand, the harder it is to take advantage of you. You don't have to know everything, but there are a few things you need to know. This is where we come in. At Paul Winkler Inc., we believe that an educated investor is a more confident investor, and a confident investor is a more successful investor.

WHAT'S THE NEXT STEP?

While you can attempt to implement these strategies on your own, it will require many years of study, research, and experience to get it right. Yes, even one mistake can cost you thousands of dollars in retirement income. It helps to have a guide. Someone who doesn't represent a big insurance company, bank, or investment product. Someone on your side who wants to see you succeed in your financial goals.

As you've seen in this guide, to be a successful investor, there are a few things you must know. If you don't, the industry *will* take advantage of you. There are just too many obstacles in the way. With a sea of investment options, and another language of jargon to learn, it's a lot to navigate on your own.

That's where we come in. We're here to guide you through those obstacles and give you peace of mind. Every aspect of our company is designed to help you relax about money.

- We don't make commissions, so you can feel confident you're not being sold something you don't need.
- We have strict education and experience requirements for our advisors, so you know you're talking to an expert.
- We use an academic approach to investing that makes sense, so you know exactly what your money is doing.

You *can* overcome the investment industry, become a confident investor in retirement, and relax about money.

Go to paulwinkler.com and schedule a call with an advisor today.

About the Author

Paul is the President and founder of Paul Winkler, Inc., a registered investment advisory firm located in Goodlettsville, Tennessee. Paul began his career in the financial services industry in 1989 through—like countless others—insurance and mutual fund sales.

After discovering the academic research on investing, he was compelled to start his own business. "With my new understanding of investing, I could no longer, in good conscience, work for the broker-dealer selling products. I wanted to offer clients an investing experience unlike what they would find elsewhere, where they wouldn't feel sold to but instead would be coached to understand investing."

Paul's differentiated approach to the world of investing and financial planning stems from his strong belief that the traditional approach to the discipline is often driven more by marketing and sales of financial products than it is by sound investment philosophies. Paul is the author of the book "Above the Maddening Crowd," which is endorsed by many financial teachers and university professors around the country.

Advisory services are offered through Paul Winkler, Inc., an SEC registered investment advisor. The opinions voiced and information provided in this material are for general informational purposes only and not intended to provide specific advice or recommendations for any individual. To determine what investments are appropriate for you, please consult with a financial advisor. PWI does not provide tax or legal advice. Please consult your tax or legal advisor regarding your particular situation.

Made in the USA
Monee, IL
05 November 2026

67380364R00029